Jonathan Swift

Gulliver

Retold and Activities by
Janet Borsbey and Ruth Swan

Illustrated by
Simone Massoni

For
Ramona Carbonari
The Prof
1985 - 2011

Young Adult (ELI) **Readers**

Young Adult Eli Readers

The **ELI Readers** collection is a complete range of
books and plays for readers of all ages, ranging from
captivating contemporary stories to timeless classics.
There are four series, each catering for a different age
group: **First ELI Readers**, **Young ELI Readers**,
Teen ELI Readers and **Young Adult ELI Readers**.
The books are carefully edited and beautifully
illustrated to capture the essence of the stories and
plots. The readers are supplemented with 'Focus on'
texts packed with background cultural information
about the writers and their lives and times.

Gulliver's Travels
Jonathan Swift
Retold and Activities
Janet Borsbey and Ruth Swan
Language Level Consultant
Silvana Sardi
Illustrations
Simone Massoni

ELI Readers
Founder and Series Editors
*Paola Accattoli, Grazia Ancillani,
Daniele Garbuglia (Art Director)*

Graphic Design
Emilia Coari

Production Manager
Francesco Capitano

Photo credits
Shutterstock

© **New edition: 2022**
First edition: 2012
ELi, Gruppo editoriale ELi
P.O. Box 6
62019 Recanati (MC)
Italy
T +39 071750701
F +39 071977851
info@elionline.com
www.elionline.com

Typeset in 10,5 / 15 pt Monotype Fulmar
Printed in Italy by Tecnostampa – Pigini
Group Printing Division
Loreto – Trevi (Italia) – ERA 102.10

ISBN 978-88-536-3222-7

Contents

GULLIVER'S WORLD

INDIA

CHINA

BROBDINGNAG

DISCOVERED A.D. 1703

BORNEO

BLEFUSCU

LILLIPUT

NEW HOLLAND

BLEFUSCU

LILLIPUT

DISCOVERED A.D. 1699

Book brief

1 This novel by Jonathan Swift, first published in 1726, is considered a classic of English literature and was an immediate success.

2 Set at the start of the 1700s, Lemuel Gulliver, an Englishman, tells the story of his travels.

3 He leaves England to visit the imaginary countries of Lilliput, Blefuscu, Brobdingnag, Laputa, and the land of the Houyhnhnms.

4 It's a satire of 18th century English society and traveller's stories which were very popular in England at that time.

5 Through the different countries that Gulliver visits, Swift tells the reader what he thinks is wrong with humans in general and, in particular, English society.

In this reader:

21st Century Skills — To encourage students to connect the story to the world they live in.

A1 MOVERS — A1 level activities.

Culture Notes — Brief cultural information.

Glossary — An explanation of difficult words.

Picture Caption — A brief explanation of the picture.

Audio — These icons indicate the parts of the story that are recorded: start ▶ stop ■

BROBDINGNAG

NORTH AMERICA

LAPUTA

BALNIBARBI

DISCOVERED A.D. 1701

LAPUTA

SOUTH SEA

OUTH SEA

HOUYHNHNMS

DISCOVERED A.D. 1711

HOUYHNHNMS

Vocabulary and Speaking

1 **Match these words to the parts of Gulliver's body.**

1 ☐ arm
2 ☐ leg
3 ☐ hand
4 ☐ mouth
5 ☐ finger
6 ☐ eye
7 ☐ nose
8 ☐ hair
9 ☐ foot
10 ☐ face

2 A Match the adjectives in box **A** with their opposites from box **B**.
Use your dictionary to help you.

A	**B**
1 ☐ beautiful	**a** lazy
2 ☐ rich	**b** sad
3 ☐ hard-working	**c** quiet
4 ☐ lucky	**d** rude
5 ☐ happy	**e** poor
6 ☐ noisy	**f** ugly
7 ☐ polite	**g** unlucky
8 ☐ hard	**h** dark
9 ☐ light	**i** soft

2 B ◆ **21st Century Skills**

Work in pairs. Use the adjectives from 2A. Describe:
- people from your family
- a person you like and say why
- a person you don't like and say why

3 Match the jobs to the dictionary definitions. Use your translation
dictionary to help you.

1 ☐ **doctor** /ˈdɒktə/
2 ☐ **engineer** /ˌendʒəˈnɪə(r)/
3 ☐ **servant** /ˈsɜː(r)v(ə)nt/
4 ☐ **soldier** /ˈsəʊldʒə(r)/
5 ☐ **sailor** /ˈseɪlə(r)/
6 ☐ **farmer** /ˈfɒː(r)mə(r)/

a someone who fights for a country
b a person who looks after ill people
c someone who works on a boat
d someone who designs buildings
e a person who grows things or keeps animals
f someone who works in someone else's home

Chapter One

I Arrive in Lilliput

Myself and my family. I decide* to travel.
Disaster* at sea. Lilliput.

▶ 2 My name is Lemuel Gulliver and this is my story.

My father came from the north of England and I was his middle son: I had two older brothers and two younger brothers. We didn't have much money, but my father sent me to Cambridge University. I was fourteen years old. I was very lucky. I studied hard, but after three years it was time for me to start work. I went to London to work for a famous doctor. In my free time, I studied more. I studied navigation*, mathematics and medicine. Why? Because I wanted to be a doctor and I wanted to travel. I finished my studies and I found a job as a doctor on a ship called the *Swallow*.

I travelled for three and a half years with the *Swallow*. After these three and a half years, I was tired, so I decided to stay in London. I found a small house and I found some patients*. I found a wife. Her name was Mary and she had £400. But life was difficult on dry land*. I was a good doctor, but I was too honest*. The rich doctors in London weren't very honest. They made a lot of money from their patients – the patients bought a lot of medicines from them. I didn't want to be like them. I had no choice*; I had to go back to sea. For the next six

Cambridge University was founded in 1209 and is the second-oldest university in the English-speaking world.

decide when you think about doing something and then you do it
disaster something terrible
navigation how to use boats at sea

patient (here) a doctor's customer
on dry land on land, not on the sea
honest (here) work well
choice when you can choose to do something

years, I travelled to the East and West Indies. I made a lot of money. On the ship, I spent my free time reading. On dry land, I watched new people and learned new languages.

I had enough money to stay at home with my wife and family. I stayed in London with them and I was happy. But, three years later, I had money problems again. I looked for another ship and found the *Antelope*. Captain William Pritchard gave me a job. I was a ship's doctor again. The *Antelope* left from Bristol on May 4th, 1699. Our destination* was the South Seas.

The journey went well, until we met a terrible storm*. The strong wind was very dangerous: we went up and down and left and right. Twelve men died in the storm. Suddenly*, the ship hit rocks near Van Diemen's Land. Disaster! The ship broke in two. Six of us jumped into a small boat. We tried to move away from the ship, but it was hard. We were near land when the wind hit our small boat. Suddenly, I was in the water! I never saw my five friends again. I swam and swam for hours and hours, until I was so tired that I couldn't swim. 'I'll die here,' I thought.

But what was *this*? Suddenly I could feel land under my feet. I felt stronger now. Now I could walk. I had to walk for a long time, before I arrived at* the shore*. It wasn't very windy now and I could see the sun. It was about eight o'clock in the evening. I walked along the beach, looking for houses or some people. I was tired and it was very hot. It was November (November 5th, I think), but that was summer in the South Seas. I decided to sit down. Then, I lay down. The sand*

The East Indies was used in the 16th century to describe countries in Southeast Asia like Indonesia, Malaysia, the Philippines and many more. The West Indies was used to describe islands like the Bahamas and the Antilles, now usually called the Caribbean.

destination the place you want to go
storm bad weather with wind and rain
suddenly quickly, as a surprise

arrive at get to, come to
shore the area between the land and the sea
sand it's yellow, it's on the beach

was warm and soft. I went to sleep. I slept for hours, I think about nine hours.

When I woke up it was light. I decided to get up and look for help. I couldn't move my legs! I tried to move my arms, but I couldn't! I tried to move my head, but I couldn't! Then I understood why. Ropes*. Thousands of little ropes were over my legs and my arms. The ropes were everywhere, even in my hair. The sun was very hot and its light hurt my eyes. Then, something moved on my leg. It moved across my body, until I could see it. It was a little man, about six inches* tall. Now I could feel another forty little men walking all over me. I shouted. They ran away. They were afraid, but so was I. They soon came back. One of them came up to my face again and shouted, '*Hekina degul!*'

His friends repeated* the words. I didn't understand their language.

I tried to move. I broke the little ropes on my left arm and tried to catch one of the little men. They ran away again and then I heard a shout, '*Tolgo Phonac!*'

Suddenly, I felt a terrible pain* in my left hand. 'They're throwing arrows*!' I thought.

Some arrows went into my hand, some into my body. I tried to free my hair. More terrible pain. Then the arrows stopped, so I tried to free my right arm. The arrows started again. 'I must stay still*,' I thought. 'I can wait until night. These people are too small to keep me here.' I was right: the arrows stopped again.

Now I could hear a lot of noise. There were more little men. 'What are they doing?' I thought. 'They're building something.' Again, I was right. Now I could see a platform* made of wood.

---

rope you use this to pull things
inch 2.54 centimetres
repeat say again
pain what you feel when something hurts you

arrow
still not moving
platform something to stand on

Jonathan Swift

The little men are putting new ropes on Gulliver and the emperor is pointing to where Gulliver can stay.

The platform was near my head on the right. After an hour, they stopped building. Some of the little men cut* the hair on my left, so I could move my head. I looked to the right. I could see four of the little men on the platform. 'They want to talk to me,' I thought.

One of the men was older and taller than the others. He started to speak, but I couldn't understand. Now I was quite hungry. I put my fingers on my mouth. The man understood. A few minutes later, I felt hundreds of the little men on my body. They had food for me. They put some in my mouth. I ate and ate. Then they brought something delicious* to drink. I drank and drank. The little men were so happy that they danced on my body. '*Hekinah degul!*' they shouted.

Then a very important man arrived. He had a letter from the emperor*. I understood from his hands, that the emperor wanted to see me. I had to go to the capital city*. I also understood that I wasn't free. Suddenly, I felt tired. Why? Sleeping medicine in the wine, they told me later. I slept for about eight hours.

When I woke up, I was in a strange* cart* on the way to the capital. It took five hundred engineers*, nine hundred strong men and fifteen hundred horses to take me there. They were very clever people. We arrived at the capital two days later. The emperor was there to meet me. 'This is your new home,' he said.

He pointed* to an old church*. Some of the men put new ropes on my legs, but now I could walk a little.

The next morning, the emperor came to see me again with his family. With him were carts of food and drink. The emperor was taller than all his countrymen and his face was strong. He was about

cut what you do with a knife
delicious very good
emperor a king
capital city most important city of a country
strange not what you usually see

cart

engineer (here) someone who designs buildings
point show with your finger

church

14

twenty-eight years old. He spoke to me, but I couldn't understand. I tried English, Dutch, Latin, French, Spanish and Italian. No-one could understand me and, after about two hours, they went away. I sat outside the church, watching some soldiers*. Suddenly, I felt an arrow near my eye. A group of six little men fired* more arrows at me. The soldiers were angry with the little men. I picked up the six men and put five of them in my pocket*. I put the other man near my mouth. Now the soldiers were worried. I put the little man down and he ran away.

'I don't eat little men!' I said, smiling.

One by one, I took the other little men out of my pocket and they all ran away. The soldiers were all very happy indeed*. The little people began to trust* me. After about two weeks, six hundred beds arrived at my new house. The little men put them all together to make one big bed. After that, I was very comfortable*.

***

Everybody in Lilliput now knew about me. Rich people, lazy people and curious* people all came to see me. The emperor often came to see me, too. He also talked to all the important people in the land. Some people were worried: my food was very expensive and I was dangerous. They wanted to kill* me. The emperor said no. He remembered the six little men who fired arrows. 'Find me the best teachers!' he said. 'This man must learn our language.'

After about three weeks, I could speak the language quite well.

---

soldier someone who fights for a country
fire shoot

pocket

(very happy) indeed very, very, very (happy)
to trust (here) think I was a good person
comfortable soft and warm
curious interested in something
kill make someone die

The emperor sometimes came to give me conversation practice. Every time he came, I asked him for my freedom*.

'Be patient*,' he always said.

I was now very comfortable with my bed, the language and some new clothes. When the men brought me my new clothes, they made a list* of all my things. Later that day, the emperor came to visit. He had thousands of soldiers with him. 'I want to take your sword*,' he said.

I took out my sword slowly. The sunlight* caught the sword. The light hurt the soldiers' eyes and they were all afraid. I put the sword on the ground* and hundreds of soldiers took it away. After that, I gave my other things to the emperor: my money, my comb* and my notebook. The soldiers took them all away. I was lucky. When they made the list of my things, they didn't find my secret pocket. In that pocket were my glasses and a pocket telescope*. I didn't tell the emperor about them. I wanted to keep them for myself.

freedom be free, so you can go where you want
be patient (here) be quiet and wait
list when you write the name of things one below the other
sword

sunlight the light from the sun
ground the floor outside
comb
telescope something which helps you see things that aren't near you

Reading Comprehension

1 **Are the sentences true (T) or false (F)?**

		T	F
1	Lemuel Gulliver is the captain of the *Swallow*.	☐	☐
2	Gulliver's wife is called Mary.	☐	☐
3	Gulliver earns a lot of money in London.	☐	☐
4	The people of Lilliput are all very small.	☐	☐
5	The people of Lilliput are afraid of Gulliver at first.	☐	☐
6	Gulliver is a free man in Lilliput.	☐	☐
7	The people of Lilliput make him a large bed.	☐	☐
8	Gulliver learns the language of Lilliput.	☐	☐
9	The emperor isn't kind to Gulliver.	☐	☐
10	Gulliver gives his glasses to the emperor.	☐	☐

Vocabulary

2 **Fill the gaps in the sentences with the words from the box.**

> ~~shore~~ - coast - rock - beach - sand - cave - port

The ......*shore*...... is the area between the beach and the sea.

1 A .... is a hole or room inside a mountain.

2 The .... is the place in a seaside town where people stop their boats.

3 In the summer, people often sit or play on the ....

4 The .... is the part of a country near the sea.

5 .... is usually golden or yellow. You often find it on a beach.

6 You often find a .... in the sea or on the beach. If there are a lot of them, they can be dangerous for ships.

Grammar and Speaking

3 A Adverbs of Frequency. Put the sentences into order of frequency. 1 is the most frequent.

a ☐ I *hardly* ever go swimming in the winter.

b ☐ I *never* sit in the sun on the beach. It's boring.

c ☑ I *always* go to the seaside in the summer.

d ☐ I *often* go skiing in the winter.

e ☐ I *usually* study hard in the winter.

f ☐ People *sometimes* visit a different country in the summer.

3 B ◆ **21st Century Skills**

Talk in pairs about the things you do in the summer and things you do in the winter. Use the adverbs.

Pre-Reading Activity • Chapter Two

Listening

▶ 3 **4 A** Listen to the beginning of Chapter Two. While you listen, write the verbs you hear.

RULES

1. The Man Mountain must not **(a)** l.......................... Lilliput without permission.

2. He must not come into the city without permission.

3. He must **(b)** s.......................... on the roads.

4. He must be careful (our people are very small).

5. He must carry urgent messages for the emperor.

6. He must **(c)** h.......................... us in our war with Blefuscu.

7. He must help us build new houses.

8. He must **(d)** m.......................... a map of our country.

9. He can **(e)** h.......................... food and drink = to 1,724 Lilliputians.

4 B Read Chapter Two and check your answers.

My Life in Lilliput

Lilliput. Freedom. War with Blefuscu.
Escape to Blefuscu. I return to England.

▶ 3 People in Lilliput seemed* more friendly now. Boys and girls played in my hair and they called me Man Mountain. The horses weren't scared* of me now. People enjoyed coming to see me: I was now a tourist attraction. One day, the emperor asked me to stand up with my feet apart*. He then told his soldiers to march* under me. Everyone enjoyed the parade*.

'Now I'll give you your freedom,' the emperor said, 'But there are some rules*. So, there are nine rules. If you agree*, you'll be free.'

The emperor gave me a piece of paper.

RULES
1. The Man Mountain must not leave Lilliput without permission*.
2. He must not come into the city without permission.
3. He must stay on the roads.
4. He must be careful (our people are very small).
5. He must carry urgent* messages for the emperor.
6. He must help us in our war with Blefuscu.
7. He must help us build new houses.
8. He must make a map of our country.
9. He can have food and drink = to 1,724 Lilliputians.

seem give the idea that
scared afraid
apart not near
march walk like a soldier
parade when people walk in a big group

rule something you must do
agree say yes, OK
permission this says you can do something
urgent very important

4 I had no problem with the rules. I asked a friend about how they decided how much food and drink to give me.

'The best mathematicians in the country decided this,' he said. 'They thought about your height – you're exactly 12 times taller than us. Your volume is therefore 12^3. As you know, 12^3 equals 1,724.'

I checked the mathematics: $12 \times 12 \times 12 = 1,724$. 'You're very clever people,' I answered, 'And very good at economics!'

In the story, Lilliput and Blefuscu are two islands in the South Indian Ocean. These empires are a satire of the Kingdom of Great Britain and the Kingdom of France in the 18th century.

***

About two weeks later, I had a visitor. His name was Reldresal and he was an important man. He sat in my hand and we talked. He told me about some of the problems in Lilliput. He was worried about political differences. He was also worried about war: war with Blefuscu. 'The biggest problem', he said, 'is eggs.'

'Eggs?' I asked, surprised.

'Yes, eggs. Big-Endians and Little-Endians.'

I was confused. 'What are Big-Endians and Little-Endians?'

'Everyone in Lilliput has boiled eggs for breakfast. In the past, everyone cut their boiled egg at the big end. They were Big-Endians. Then, an emperor cut his finger. He made a law*: everyone had to cut their boiled egg at the little end. We became Little-Endians. Some people changed, but other people didn't. There were protests*. Some Big-Endians left Lilliput. Today, there are still problems. The Emperor of Blefuscu helps the Big-Endians. So, we're at war with Blefuscu – about eggs.'

The problem between the Big-Endians and Little Endians is Swift's way of talking about religious problems in Britain. In the 1530s, King Henry VIII made new laws and many people in the country became Protestants and left the Catholic church.

'Can I help?' I asked.

'I hope so,' answered Reldresal sadly. 'The Emperor of Blefuscu

law an official rule

protest when people show they're angry about something

has a lot of ships. He has more than us and the ships are ready to attack* us.'

'Let me speak to the emperor,' I said. I had an idea.

***

The Empire of Blefuscu is very near to Lilliput. The channel* between the two countries is less than a mile* wide and the water isn't very deep. Before I went to see the emperor, I went to the beach. I looked at the Blefuscu ships through my pocket telescope. There were about fifty ships. I went quickly to the palace*. I told the emperor my idea and he was very happy indeed. I went home to prepare* some small ropes.

The next morning, I went to the shore. I took off my coat and my shoes and swam across the channel. When I got near to the Emperor of Blefuscu's ships, his soldiers were scared. Some of them jumped into the water. Some of them fired arrows at me and I was worried about my eyes. Then I remembered my glasses and put them on. My job was very easy: I put ropes on all the Emperor of Blefuscu's ships. Then I pulled them across the channel to Lilliput.

The Emperor of Lilliput was very happy. He gave me a special reward* – I was a Nardac (like a lord, dear reader)! The emperor was so happy that he decided to send me to Blefuscu again. 'You can kill all the Big-Endians!' he said. 'Everyone will cut their eggs from the little end, everyone in the world! I'll be emperor of the whole* world!'

'No! That's not right,' I shouted. 'I can't help you. I don't want to kill people. I don't want to kill people because of eggs!'

The emperor was surprised and then he was angry.

attack hurt someone
channel (here) water
mile 1.609 kilometres
palace where a king lives

prepare get ready
reward a gift to say 'well done'
whole complete, all

'Don't trust the emperor,' my friend said later that evening. 'Some of the emperor's friends are angry with you. You're a Nardac and they want to be Nardacs. They'll say bad things about you. The emperor will change.'

'I'll be very careful. You can't always trust emperors,' I said.

A few weeks later, the most important Blefuscans came to Lilliput. 'We must end the war,' they said to the emperor, 'We don't want to fight anymore. It's time for us to be friends.'

The Emperor of Lilliput said yes. The Emperor of Blefuscu had to pay a lot of money, but the war was over. There was a big dinner to celebrate* the end of the war. At the dinner, I met the Emperor of Blefuscu. I liked him and I talked to him for a long time. I was lucky, he was very important to me later.

***

Now that I was a Nardac, life was different. I didn't build houses now. I had time to learn more about Lilliput. I talked to a lot of people and I learned to write Lilliputian. This was very difficult. Lilliputian writing isn't from left to right like Europeans. It isn't from right to left like Arabic writers. It's diagonal*, from one corner of the paper to the other. There are many other differences. For example, Lilliputians believe* that the Earth is flat*. They also have some very strict* laws.

I lived very well in Lilliput. I had three hundred cooks, twenty waiters and lots and lots of other servants*. People began to talk. They said I was very expensive. Many of the emperor's friends were angry with me. They began to talk to the emperor. My friend was right – the Emperor of Lilliput began to change.

---

celebrate have a party to remember a happy day
diagonal

believe think that something is true
flat level, not round
strict strong, hard
servant someone who works in someone else's home

Gulliver is pulling the
ship across the channel.

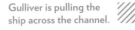

'He didn't want to fight for us,' one said.

'He talked to the Emperor of Blefuscu,' said another.

'He wants to live in Blefuscu,' said a third man.

'Oh no! You're right,' said the emperor, 'He'll fight against us! We must kill him.'

Later that night, my good friend came to see me. 'You must leave Lilliput,' he said.

'I know,' I answered. 'It's too dangerous for me here.'

We made a plan.

***

That night, I said goodbye to my Lilliputian friend. I swam to Blefuscu. I took a ship and put my things in it. I pulled the ship across the channel with me. The people of Blefuscu were very pleased to see me. They sent a message to the Emperor of Blefuscu. Almost immediately, the emperor and his wife arrived at the shore. The people of Blefuscu were *not* scared of me.

The emperor was very kind* to me, but there was one problem: there was no house for me in Blefuscu, so I slept outside.

Three days later, I went for a walk. I went to the north-east of the island. I saw something in the sea. Was it a boat? I took off my coat and shoes and swam to it. It was a boat. An empty* boat and it was my size*. I swam back to the shore and went immediately to the city. I asked for a meeting with the emperor. He was happy to see me.

'Your Majesty*,' I began, 'I need your help.'

'I'll help you, if I can,' he answered.

'Thank you, your Majesty. I need twenty ships and three thousand men.'

---

kind nice, good
empty with nothing in it
size (here) right for him to travel in

Your Majesty you can use this when you speak to a king

The emperor was surprised. 'Why?'

'There's a big boat in the sea in the north-east. I need your help to bring it here. I can use the boat to return to my country.'

The emperor was very kind. He gave me the ships and the men. We brought the boat back to Blefuscu.

Before I left, the emperor got a letter from Lilliput. The Emperor of Lilliput was very, very angry. 'Send the Man Mountain back to Lilliput,' he wrote.

The Emperor of Blefuscu sent a letter back. 'I'm very sorry,' he wrote, 'but I can't send him back to you. The Man Mountain is very kind. He is a peaceful* man. He stopped the war between us.'

The emperor showed me his letter. He asked me to stay in Blefuscu. 'I'll protect* you,' he said.

'No, I must leave,' I answered.

The emperor helped me. He gave me food and drink for the journey*. He also gave me some money. I took some of the little animals with me to show people at home. I wanted to take some of the little men with me too, but the emperor said no.

On 24th September, 1701, at six in the morning, I left Blefuscu.

***

My journey was very comfortable. The first day, the weather was good. I stopped near a small island and slept for a few hours. The next day was the same. On the third day, at about three o'clock in the afternoon, I saw a ship. To my surprise, the ship was English. I reached* the ship about two hours later. The captain* was a very kind man.

peaceful a peaceful person doesn't want war
protect help someone to stay safe
journey the time you travel

reach arrive at
captain the head of the ship

'Where are you going?' I asked.

'England,' he answered. 'We are returning from Japan.'

Everyone on the ship was curious about my story. They didn't believe that the people on Lilliput were so small. 'You're mad*!' they said.

'Let me show you something,' I answered.

I showed them my little animals. Now, they believed me.

The journey was very comfortable and we soon arrived home. I made a lot of money with my little animals. I took them to markets in London and I showed them to people. People paid a lot to see them. Then someone bought them for a hundred pounds. Now I was rich.

***

I stayed with my wife and family and I bought a new house. But I didn't want to stay in England, I wanted to travel. I gave my wife fifteen hundred pounds. I said goodbye to her, my son and my daughter. We were all very sad. I left England again. The name of my ship was the *Adventure*. I'll tell you all about my adventures* on the *Adventure* in the next chapter.

---

mad not thinking right   **adventure** something exciting that you do

After-Reading Activities • Chapter Two

Reading Comprehension

1 Choose the best answer A, B or C.

1 What do the Lilliputian boys and girls do?
- ☐ **A** They play in Gulliver's hair.
- ☐ **B** They fire arrows at him.
- ☐ **C** They march with the army.

2 Why does the Emperor of Lilliput call mathematicians?
- ☐ **A** To help make a map.
- ☐ **B** To help build houses.
- ☐ **C** To decide how much food and drink to give to Gulliver.

3 Why is Lilliput at war with Blefuscu?
- ☐ **A** Because of the way they eat eggs.
- ☐ **B** Because of the way they cut eggs.
- ☐ **C** Because they don't like eggs.

4 How many ships does Gulliver take from the Emperor of Blefuscu?
- ☐ **A** 30
- ☐ **B** 40
- ☐ **C** 50

5 Why does the Emperor of Lilliput make Gulliver a Nardac?
- ☐ **A** To thank him.
- ☐ **B** To help him.
- ☐ **C** To make life difficult for him.

6 Why does the emperor get angry with Gulliver?
- ☐ **A** Gulliver wants to be the emperor.
- ☐ **B** Gulliver wants to keep the ships.
- ☐ **C** Gulliver doesn't want to kill anyone.

7 What does Gulliver take with him to England?
- ☐ **A** Six little men.
- ☐ **B** Six little animals.
- ☐ **C** Six little emperors.

Grammar

2 **Choose the right words (A, B or C) to complete the text about Chapter Two.**

The Lilliputs enjoyed ......*coming*.... to see Gulliver and the horses weren't scared of **(1)** .... anymore. Gulliver thought that they were very good **(2)** .... maths and he had lots to eat. Reldresal told Gulliver about **(3)** .... of the problems in Lilliput because he was worried about war with Blefuscu. The Emperor of Lilliput was happy when Gulliver **(4)** .... the Emperor of Blefuscu's ships to Lilliput. Then Gulliver **(5)** .... to leave Lilliput because it was too dangerous to stay there.

	A come	**B** ~~coming~~	**C** to come
1	**A** he	**B** is	**C** him
2	**A** at	**B** in	**C** to
3	**A** any	**B** some	**C** none
4	**A** bring	**B** brought	**C** brings
5	**A** could	**B** must	**C** had

Pre-Reading Activity • Chapter Three

Speaking

3 A **In Chapter Three, Gulliver travels to a country where he's small and everyone is very big. What problems will he have there? Tick the boxes. Tell your partner your reasons.**

a ☐ It'll be difficult to leave the country.

b ☐ People will be unkind to him.

c ☐ People will put him in a zoo.

d ☐ Insects will attack him.

e ☐ Children will try to eat him.

f ☐ Big people will be noisy.

g ☐ It'll be difficult to cross the road.

3 B **Read Chapter Three and check your answers.**

Chapter Three

My Journey to Brobdingnag

I go back to sea. I arrive at the land of giants.
I become a tourist attraction.
I live with the king and queen.

5 On 20th June, 1702, I left England on the *Adventure*. We had a very good journey south and stopped for the winter at the Cape of Good Hope. In the spring, we sailed* again. We saw Madagascar and sailed towards* the Molucca Islands. The weather was very good. Too good. Captain Nicholas was a very good sailor*. He understood weather. 'There will be a terrible storm tomorrow. A monsoon*,' he said one day.

He was right. It was stormy for many days. No-one knew where we were. We had lots of food, but we didn't have much water. We started to look for land.

On 16th June, 1703, we saw land. Some of us got into a small boat and went towards the shore. When we arrived, we started to look for water. Some of us went left and others went right. I didn't see any people and I didn't find any water. I was tired, so I started to go back to the boat. When I got back to the shore, I couldn't see the boat. Then, I saw it. At sea, moving quickly. Behind it, there was a very tall man. A giant*. He tried but couldn't catch the boat. I ran away.

sail travel in a boat using the wind
towards to
sailor someone who works on a boat

monsoon tropical bad weather
giant a very big person

I ran for miles. I arrived at a field*. The field was full of wheat*, but it was very, very tall. Suddenly, another giant man appeared*, then another, then a woman. There were seven of them.

'What are they doing?' I thought. 'They're farmers. Oh, no! They're cutting the wheat!'

I ran and ran, but the farmers came nearer. I stopped, very tired. 'My wife,' I thought. 'My poor wife and my poor children. Why did I leave England? I don't want to die here!'

I thought about Lilliput and the little people. They were scared of me. Now I was scared of someone much bigger than me. At that very moment, I saw a foot. 'No! Help! Stop!' I shouted, loudly.

The farmer stopped. He looked at the ground in front of him. Then he saw me. He looked at me for a while*. I understood his thoughts. I look like this when I see a strange animal. 'Will it hurt me?' I think.

After a while, he picked me up, carefully. He held me between his thumb* and a finger. I was scared. I was very high in the air. 'Don't drop me!' I shouted. 'Ouch! You're hurting me!'

He seemed to understand. The farmer put me into his pocket. He walked towards his friends. 'Look at this!' I think he said. I didn't understand the language, but I could guess. The farmer put me on the ground. His friends sat down in a circle. They watched me. I tried to talk to them. I tried many different languages. They couldn't really hear me and they couldn't understand. The farmers tried to talk to me, but the noise was very loud. It hurt my ears.

After a while, the farmer carried me to his house. He was very careful. He called his wife. She was scared and ran away. She came back after a minute or two and was very kind to me. It was lunchtime

---

field a place where farmers grow things
wheat farmers grow this, we use it to make bread

appear if something appears, we can see it
a while some time
thumb you have four fingers and one thumb on each hand

The giant is holding Gulliver
between his thumb and a finger.

and she put a very big plate onto the table. The family came to eat. They were very curious. In total, there were the farmer and his wife, their three children and an old grandmother. The farmer's wife gave me some food and drink. Suddenly, a giant cat jumped up to sit on the wife's knees. I was scared for a moment, but I think the cat was more afraid of me.

After lunch, the nurse came into the room with the farmer's enormous* baby. This was a terrible moment. The baby saw me and immediately picked me up. He put me into his mouth. I was very lucky: the farmer's wife pulled my legs and I was free. Then, the farmer's wife took me upstairs and put me into a bedroom. She locked the door. I slept for about two hours. When I woke up, I looked around the room. Then I saw them, two enormous rats*. They wanted to eat me! I took out my sword and killed the first one. The second ran away. The farmer's wife came in at that moment and saved* me.

***

I liked the farmer's daughter very much. She was nine years old and about forty feet* tall. She made a little bed for me. She also made seven little shirts for me. She was my teacher, too. Very quickly, I began to understand their language. She called me Grildrig – little man. Everyone in the family then called me Grildrig. Soon, everyone in the country called me Grildrig. Her name was Glumdalclitch and she was very, very kind to me. Glumdalclitch stayed with me all the time I was in Brobdingnag.

Everyone in the village knew about me. I was a strange animal, just like a human but very small. When visitors came to the house, the farmer put me on the table. I spoke to the people in their language.

enormous very, very big

rat

save stop someone from dying
forty feet about 12 metres

One visitor said to the farmer. 'Put him in a box and take him to the market. People will pay to see him,' he said.

Glumdalclitch was afraid. 'Don't hurt him!' she said.

The next day, the farmer put me in a box to take me to the market. Glumdalclitch came with us. The journey was uncomfortable in my little box. When we arrived at the village, the farmer found a room at a hotel. He brought people to see me. Glumdalclitch asked me questions and I answered in their language. A schoolboy threw a peanut* at me. It didn't hit me: I was very lucky.

The farmer was very happy. He decided to take me to all the markets in Brobdingnag.

***

Travelling was very difficult for me and very uncomfortable. I became ill. The farmer wasn't worried. 'Someone must buy him before he dies,' he thought.

Luckily, a message came from the queen*. She wanted to see me immediately, so we went to the palace. She was very kind. 'Where are you from?' she asked.

'England,' I answered.

'And why did you come to Brobdingnag?'

I told her about my travels. The queen was very interested. She decided to buy me. 'How much must I give you?' she asked the farmer.

'A thousand gold pieces,' he answered.

'Your Majesty,' I said.

'Yes, Grildrig?'

'I have one question. Can Glumdalclitch come too? She's my nurse and my teacher.'

peanut   queen

Glumdalclitch was happy, the queen was happy and the farmer was happy. He was rich and his daughter lived in the royal palace.

One day, the queen took me to see her husband, the king. He was surprised. 'Is that your new pet?' he asked. 'What is it?'

'He's not an animal!' she answered. 'Listen.'

The queen asked me some questions and I answered in her language. The king was interested in my story, too. He called Glumdalclitch. 'Is his story true?' he asked.

'Yes,' she answered.

At first the king wasn't sure*. Perhaps* I was a clockwork* toy. So he called the three most intelligent people in Brobdingnag. They looked at me and they talked to me.

'He isn't an animal. He isn't fast and he can't climb trees,' one said.

'He isn't a man,' said another. 'He's too small.'

'He's a freak*. A freak of nature,' they all said.

'Your Majesty!' I shouted. 'I'm a man. I come from a country called England. In England there are millions of men and women like me. In my country, the trees and the animals are in proportion* to us.'

The three intelligent people laughed at me.

***

The king was a fair* man. He was still interested in my story. 'Look after him,' he said to the queen. 'Give him food, build a house for him. I like him.'

The queen called a carpenter*. 'Make a beautiful house for this man,' she said.

The carpenter was very clever. He made a very comfortable box

---

not sure (here) not understand what something is and if it's good or bad
perhaps we say perhaps when we're not sure about something
clockwork mechanical, (here) a moving toy

freak (here) an unusual person
proportion (here) the right size for people
fair right, correct
carpenter a person who makes things with wood like chairs and tables

for me. It had windows, a bed, chairs, a table and a wardrobe*. It was perfect for travelling and for living.

The queen liked me. I always had dinner with her. She found toy silver plates, knives and forks for me and she cut my food for me.

Every Wednesday (Wednesdays were holidays), the king and queen had lunch together. The king liked talking to me. He talked about my country and Europe. He asked about government*, laws, religion and education. Sometimes he laughed, but he *always* listened.

***

Sometimes life in Brobdingnag was dangerous for a little man. One day, I opened my window and there were twenty giant wasps* outside. Luckily, I had my sword. They attacked me, so I killed them all – one by one. I kept some wasp stings* as souvenirs*. I had problems with giant flies* too.

I often travelled with the king and queen. Brobdingnag was a very big country. European map-makers are very bad: they think there is no big country between Japan and California! 'When I return to England, I'll correct their maps,' I thought.

The mountains in the north of Brobdingnag are thirty miles high. People catch fish in the rivers not in the sea. Why? Because the fish in the sea are too small. In fact, they're just like ours in England. There are fifty-one cities in Brobdingnag and lots of villages. The cities are very beautiful and there are a lot of royal palaces and temples*.

***

wardrobe where you put your clothes
government the people who make the laws in a country
wasp

sting a wasp uses this to hurt people
souvenir something you buy to remember your holiday
fly
temple a religious building

The king began to trust me. He often asked questions about England.

'We have two islands. And we have some land in another country – America,' I said. 'We have a king and a Parliament. Parliament has two houses; the House of Lords and the House of Commons. We also have judges*. We pay tax* to the government. We have very good soldiers and very good sailors.'

'Why do you need soldiers?' he asked. 'Soldiers are very expensive. Farmers are better for the country.'

'We're a very powerful* country,' I said. 'We have very good guns*. We can kill a lot of people in a very short time. So, we stay powerful. I can help you make guns like ours.'

The king was very angry. 'No!' he shouted. 'I love science and I love art. My people study mathematics, philosophy, history and poetry. I think you're *horrible** people. You make war on other countries for power. I don't make war on other countries. I don't need big guns to kill other people. I need farmers to grow food for them.'

We didn't speak about England again.

The first British colony was founded in Jamestown, Virginia in 1607.

The Parliament of Great Britain was formed in May 1707 when the two Parliaments of England and Scotland came together to become one Parliament.

---

judge a person who decides if someone is right or wrong
tax money you must give to the government
powerful very strong

gun
horrible terrible

Vocabulary   A1 MOVERS

1 Look at the pictures and choose the correct word to write on each line.

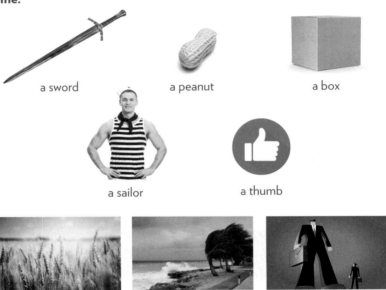

a sword   a peanut   a box

a sailor   a thumb

wheat   a storm   ~~a giant~~

This person is enormous.	*a giant*
1 You use this to make bread.	....
2 Gulliver killed some rats with this.	....
3 This person works on a ship.	....
4 A carpenter made this a nice place for Gulliver to live in.	....
5 This is part of your hand.	....
6 A schoolboy threw this at Gulliver.	....
7 Very bad weather.	....

Reading Comprehension

2 Answer the questions about Chapter Three.

1 Why do the other sailors leave Gulliver on the island?

....

....

2 What are the first two animals to attack Gulliver?

....

....

3 Why does the farmer take Gulliver to markets?

....

....

4 Who's Glumdalclitch?

....

....

5 Why don't the giants catch fish in the sea?

....

....

6 What does the king think about England?

....

....

Pre-Reading Activity · Chapter Four

Listening

▶ 6 **3 Listen to the beginning of Chapter Four. Are the sentences true (T) or false (F)?**

		T	F
1	Gulliver wanted to be free.	☐	☐
2	Gulliver travelled to the south with Glumdalclitch.	☐	☐
3	Glumdalclitch was angry with Gulliver.	☐	☐
4	Gulliver went to the sea in his box.	☐	☐
5	A giant fish attacked Gulliver.	☐	☐
6	Gulliver fell into the sea with his box.	☐	☐

Chapter Four

I Travel to Laputa

I leave Brobdingnag. I return to England.
I meet pirates. I visit the flying island of Laputa.

6 After two years in Brobdingnag, I began to think about my freedom. It seemed impossible: everyone was so big and I was so small. At the beginning of the third year, the king and queen decided to travel to the south coast*. They wanted to visit their people there. I travelled with them, in my now very comfortable box. Glumdalclitch came too. At the end of our journey to the south, Glumdalclitch and I were very tired. I had a cold and Glumdalclitch was very ill. I wanted to go outside, but Glumdalclitch wanted to sleep. She called a boy. 'Take Grildrig to the sea,' she said. 'I don't feel very well, so I'll stay here. Be very careful. Look after Grildrig well.'

Glumdalclitch was very sad. Perhaps she could see into the future.

The boy carried me (in my box) down to the sea. It took about half an hour. I was very tired and I fell asleep. I don't really know what happened next. Perhaps the boy went swimming. Perhaps he put the box down just for a minute, but suddenly I woke up.

'What's this? Why is the box moving so fast?' I thought.

I was scared. I looked out of my window. I could see the sky and clouds. I was now very high in the sky. I was in the claws* of a giant bird.

'It knows I'm in here. It'll eat me!' I thought, afraid.

---

coast the part of a country near the sea   **claw** the hands of a bird

'Help!' I shouted out of the window. 'Help!'

Suddenly, the box began to fall. It fell down and down. With a splash*, it fell into the sea.

***

7 In the water, in the box, I thought about poor Glumdalclitch. I thought about the king and queen. 'Please don't be angry with Glumdalclitch,' I said to myself.

Then I thought: 'Will someone rescue* me? Will I die in the water, here?'

After about four scary* hours, I heard a noise. It was a ship! 'Help! Help!' I shouted.

'Who's there?' A man asked in English.

'Lemuel Gulliver!' I shouted. 'Help me, please!'

The ship's carpenter cut the box open and I walked out. The sailors were very surprised. They seemed small to me. Was I back in Lilliput? No, they were the same size as me!

***

The destination of the ship was England. On the journey, I spent a lot of time with the captain. I told him about Brobdingnag. He didn't believe me. 'You're mad,' he said.

Luckily, I had the wasp sting and some other souvenirs of Brobdingnag. When he saw them, he believed my story. 'Write a book about it!' he said.

'Perhaps I will,' I answered.

I arrived home on 3rd June 1703, about nine months later. My wife was very happy to see me. My wife and my daughter seemed very small to me.

---

splash the sound something makes when it falls into water

rescue save

scary something which makes you afraid

'You'll never go to sea again!' she said.

She was wrong.

***

Ten days later, a man came to my house. His name was William Robinson and he was the captain of the Hopewell. He was like a brother to me. He came to visit me often. One day, he said, 'I want to go to India. Will you come with me? I need a good ship's doctor.'

'Yes!' I said. 'I'll be very happy to come with you.'

On 5th August 1706, we left England again. In April the next year, we arrived in Madras. We stayed there for a few weeks, because some sailors were ill. When we set off* again, there was a terrible storm. We didn't know where we were. On the tenth day, pirates saw our ship. Some of the pirates were Dutch and some were Japanese. I spoke Dutch quite well so I said, 'Please, take the ship, but don't kill us.'

The Japanese pirate was angry. 'Put him in a canoe*, alone*!' he said. 'Let him die at sea!'

The pirates took our sailors onto their ship. They put me into a canoe. I was alone, at sea, again. When I was a long way from the pirate ship, I took out my pocket telescope. Through it I saw some small islands. I sailed towards the first island, but it was very rocky. I found some eggs, ate them and slept under a rock. The next day, I sailed to another island, then another. On the 5th day, I arrived at the last island. I found some more eggs. On this island, there was a small cave*. I slept a little. I was quite worried now. I was very tired. 'Will I die here?' I thought.

When I left the cave, it was quite late the next morning. The sun was hot and the sky was clear. Suddenly, it went quite dark. I looked

There were thousands of pirates between 1650 and 1730, and these years are known as the 'Golden Age' of piracy.

set off start a journey
canoe a small, long boat

alone with no other people
cave a house inside a rock or a mountain

42

up. There was a large cloud in the sky. But no, it wasn't a cloud. What was it? It started to come down. I took out my pocket telescope. I could see people on it. It was a very big island in the sky.

I was happy to see people, so I waved* and waved. Some people on the island saw me. The island came down more. More people on the island in the sky came to look. They waved at me. The island was now very near to me.

'Help me! Help me!' I shouted.

The next minute, I saw a seat* on a rope. The seat came down from the island towards me. I sat on the seat and the people on the island pulled me up.

***

On the island in the sky, I saw some very strange people. Their eyes looked in different directions*. Their clothes had a lot of drawings on them: suns, moons, stars and musical instruments. They seemed very distracted*. Their servants told them when to speak and when to listen. The people on the island were very kind. They took me to the royal palace immediately. The king was also very kind. He sat on a chair in the middle of the room. There were mathematical instruments all around him. He asked me some questions but, of course, I didn't understand his language. Then, dinner arrived.

The food was very strange. The lamb* was triangular*, the bread was conical* and the sausages looked like musical instruments. A group of musicians played some music. I didn't like the music at all – it was terrible. After dinner, the king sent me away with a man.

---

wave move your hand to say hello or goodbye
seat a place where you sit
directions left, right
distracted when you can't think well

lamb the meat of a young sheep
triangular △
conical ◭

He had pens and paper. He was my language teacher. He taught me the names of the shapes, the moon and stars and all the musical instruments. After a few days, I began to understand the language.

***

The name of the island in the sky is Laputa. Laputa flies over a larger island under it. The name of this island is Balnibarbi. The capital city, Lagado, is on Balnibarbi. The houses on Laputa are all very strange: there are no 90° angles* in the houses. This is because the Laputans aren't practical*. They're interested in mathematics, music and astrology. The men of Laputa are also very scared. They're afraid that, one day, a falling star will hit their island. The women of Laputa live a comfortable life, but they're very bored.

The king uses physics to control the movement of Laputa. He also uses Laputa to control the people of Balnibarbi. Dear reader, the people of Balnibarbi are very oppressed*. The king can use Laputa to stop rain and block* the sun. If the people of Balnibarbi cause a lot of trouble*, the people of Laputa throw rocks at them.

***

The people on the island of Laputa were kind to me, but they weren't curious about me at all. I was quite interested in both mathematics and music, but the men were quite boring. I began to talk to the women, children and servants. The Laputan men were surprised at this, but the women, children and servants talked about more interesting things than the men. I studied hard and now I could speak their language very well. But there was nothing for me here. After two months on the island, I wanted to leave.

The 18th century was also called the Age of Reason or the Enlightenment as it was a period of great progress in science.

---

angle where two lines meet
practical realistic, sensible
oppressed treated badly by a king

block (here) stop the light from the sun by putting the island in front of it
cause a lot of trouble make problems

There was one Laputan man I liked. He was a very important lord. He was very intelligent, very practical and very interested in the world around him. Everyone said he was stupid*. Why? Because he didn't like Laputan music. He often came to talk to me in my room. 'What's Europe like? What laws are there in England? What's Lilliput like? What's Brobdingnag like?' he asked.

One day, we talked about travelling. 'Could you help me?' I asked him.

'How?' he answered.

'Will you talk to the king for me? I want to leave. I want to travel to Balnibarbi and to other places in the world.'

'Yes, I'll talk to the king,' he said.

On the 16th February, I left Laputa. The king gave me a present; some money to help me on Balnibarbi. The island of Laputa went down in the sky. When we were near Balnibarbi, I went down on the seat on the rope.

■

stupid not clever

Reading Comprehension

1 **Correct the false information in this text about Chapter Four. There are five mistakes.**

When Gulliver falls into the sea, some Japanese sailors save him. He arrives home in England nine weeks later. He stays in England for a while and then he leaves again. This time, pirates attack his ship. They put Gulliver in a canoe with a friend. Gulliver finds a small island and then sees another island in the sky. The people on the island help him to go up to Laputa. The people of Laputa are very practical and very interested in mathematics. After two months on the island, Gulliver doesn't want to leave.

2 **Answer the questions. Use short answers.**

Does Gulliver visit his wife in England? ....*Yes, he does.*............................

1   Is Gulliver happy to see his wife again? ....

2   Is William Robinson a doctor? ....

3   Are the pirates kind to Gulliver? ....

4   Do Laputans like music? ....

Grammar

3 A **Sequencing. Put these events from Chapter Four in order.**

1 ☐ ...., English sailors rescue Gulliver.

2 ☐ ...., he visits the island of Laputa.

3 ☐ ...., Gulliver goes back to England.

4 ☐ ...., Gulliver travels to the south coast.

5 ☐ ...., he goes back to sea.

3 B **Put the words from the box into the sentences. More than one answer is possible.**

First - After that - Then - Next - Finally

Writing and Speaking ◆ **21st Century Skills**

4 A Write about your favourite place to visit.

> I love .... It is ....
> I go there/I went there ....
> I love it because ....
> ....

4 B Talk in pairs. Ask and answer questions about your favourite places.

Pre-Reading Activity • Chapter Five

Speaking

5 Here are some events from Chapter Five. Why do they happen?
Choose A or B and discuss your answers in pairs.

1 Gulliver is surprised about Lagado, the capital of Balnibarbi
☐ **A** because it's very dirty.
☐ **B** because the houses are very badly built.

2 Gulliver thinks the people of Balnibarbi are poor and unhappy
☐ **A** because they don't like Laputa.
☐ **B** because their professors have silly ideas.

3 Gulliver enjoys the Magical Island
☐ **A** because he can meet people from the past.
☐ **B** because the king is good at magic tricks.

4 *Immortals* are unhappy
☐ **A** because they live for ever.
☐ **B** because they don't live for ever.

Chapter Five

I Visit Strange and Wonderful Places

On Balnibarbi. Inside the Academy.
The Magical Island. I meet Hannibal.

▶ 8　When I reached Balnibarbi, I was very happy. I walked to Lagado (I'm sure you remember that this is the capital city). I had the name of a man to visit in Lagado, Lord Munodi. He was a friend of my friend on Laputa. The man was very happy to meet me. I stayed in his house.

The next morning, he took me to visit the capital. It was about the same size as London. The houses were very strange and very badly built. The people in the streets walked fast. They looked a little wild*. Their clothes were old. Then, we walked into the countryside. Again the people were poor. I was surprised, because the land was good. Lord Munodi's house was different from the others. His garden was also more beautiful than the others. I asked Lord Munodi why.

'About forty years ago, the Laputan government built an academy here in Lagado. The academy studies building, agriculture* and languages. The professors* have some very strange ideas. They tell the Laputan government their ideas and the government makes stupid laws. They aren't practical. My house is different, because I break the laws.'

wild (here) natural, uncontrolled, untidy　　　　**professor** teacher
agriculture farming

50

'Can I visit the academy?' I asked.

'Yes, but you must go alone,' he answered. 'I hate* the academy and I'll never, ever go there. You must take some money with you. They never have any money for their studies so they beg* from visitors.

The following day, I visited the academy. The dean* was very happy to meet me. The academy was very big with about five hundred rooms.

In the first room, there was an old man. He told me about his studies. 'I'm working on a very important project. I'm trying to make sunlight from cucumbers*. We take the sunlight out of the cucumbers, put it in a bottle and then we can use it on cold days.'

Swift uses satire here to show that he thought many inventions were useless and were only done to make money.

'Very interesting,' I said. I gave him some money.

I went into another room. The smell* was so bad that I left immediately.

In another room, there was a very clever engineer. He had a new way of building houses. He built the roof* first and the walls second. At the end, he built the foundations*.

In the next room, there was a man who couldn't see. His job was to mix colours for artists. He did this by smell and by touch*.

I visited a lot of rooms in the academy, but I didn't see any practical ideas. The dean wanted to show me more rooms on the other side of the academy. There, I visited the school of languages. There were three professors there. Their job was to improve* their language.

'What exactly are you doing?' I asked one professor.

'This is my language machine,' he answered. 'It's making our words shorter. All words will soon be very, very short.'

---

hate not like
beg ask for money
dean the head teacher
cucumber a long green salad vegetable
smell you smell things with your nose

roof the top part of a building
foundations the bottom part of a building (under it)
touch you touch things with your hand
improve make better

'Very interesting,' I said.

'My job is *more* interesting,' said the second professor. 'There's no need for words in our language. Speaking is very bad for people. Too much speaking makes people ill. In my system*, we don't need words, we need *things*. People will soon communicate* by carrying things in their pockets. For short conversations, you only need a few things. Of course, for long conversations, you need servants to carry your things. For very long conversations, you need a cart. My system has one great advantage* – it's a universal language. You can communicate with people from all over the world.'

'But my language machine is the best!' said the first professor.

'No, yours is too complicated*!' said the second.

I gave them some money and left quickly.

Next, I spent a very short time at the school of mathematics. There, the scientists wrote formulas on edible* paper. They then ate them, immediately.

I now understood that all these professors were mad. Balnibarbi was poor and unhappy because of these professors and their silly ideas. I decided to leave the academy and Balnibarbi as soon as possible. I wanted to go back to Europe.

***

The next day, I spoke to Lord Munodi. 'I want to go back to England,' I said.

'I'm not surprised,' he answered. 'Perhaps I can help. The King of Luggnagg is a good friend of the Emperor of Japan. It must be possible to get from there to Japan and from Japan to England. Why don't you go to Luggnagg? It's a small island and it's quite near.'

system how you do something
communicate understand each other
advantage something good about a thing

complicated difficult to understand
edible you can eat something edible

'Thank you,' I said. 'That's a very good idea.

I said goodbye to Lord Munodi and left Lagado. I travelled to the port* of Maldonada. When I arrived, I spoke to a man at the port. 'When's the next ship for Luggnagg?' I asked.

'In five weeks,' he answered.

I decided to spend the time visiting a different island, Glubbdubdrib. Its other name is the Magical Island. It's a very small island. The king of the Magical Island is a magician*. He has a very special power. He can call ghosts* from the past to be his servants. They can only work for him for twenty-four hours. When I arrived at the Magical Island, I went immediately to see the king. He was very happy to see me and invited me to stay in the royal palace. It was a little strange at first, the servants were always different.

One evening, the king invited me to a special dinner. After dinner, we talked.

'I like you, Gulliver,' he said. 'I have an interesting idea. Do you want to meet some people from the past?'

'Yes, please!' I answered.

'Who?'

'Let me think. Alexander the Great,' I answered.

'Call him! Then he'll appear!' said the king.

'Alexander the Great!' I called.

Two seconds later, Alexander appeared. It was difficult to understand his Greek at first.

'Another!' said the king.

Soon, Hannibal appeared.

'Look! He's crossing the Alps!' I shouted.

port where ships wait before sailing   **ghost**

magician

I then asked to see Caesar and Pompey. Then the whole Senate of Rome appeared. Caesar and Brutus came near to me. I spoke to Brutus, a very fine man.

The next day, I decided to call some more ghosts. Homer and Aristotle were interesting. I called Descartes and Gassendi. Aristotle was pleased to meet them. 'Oh dear, I made some mistakes in my philosophy,' he said, after a long conversation.

The next day, I called some ghosts from modern history. They were very disappointing. I called people from the past and recent past. It was strange, all the people from the recent past were *very* disappointing. At the end of my stay on the Magical Island, I understood more about the problems of my country and the problems of Europe.

***

It was time for me to leave. I thanked the King of the Magical Island very much and went back to Maldonada. There, I found a ship for Luggnagg. The journey took a month.

It's easy to communicate with the people of Luggnagg, because many of them speak the language of Balnibarbi. The Luggnaggians are very polite*, kind people. They all seem to be very happy.

Soon after I arrived, the king invited me to the royal palace. I wanted to be polite too, so I learned some words in Luggnaggian. When I arrived at the palace, I said these words to the king, 'Ickpling gloffthrob squutserumm blhiop mlashnalt zwin modbalkguffh slhiophad gurdlubh asht.'

He was very pleased. He invited me to stay in the royal palace. I stayed for three months.

One day, a Luggnaggian asked me a strange question. 'Would you like to meet an *Immortal*?'

polite nice to people

55

'What do you mean?'

'Some people here are immortal – they live for ever.'

'How wonderful,' I said. 'Yes, I'd like to learn from an Immortal. They'll teach me a lot about life. Perhaps I can learn something special.'

Unfortunately, the Immortals aren't nice people. They're angry, horrible, jealous*, miserable* and talk a lot. Because they're different from other people, they don't have friends. They're also very ugly. They've a strange blue spot* on their heads. The oldest Immortal I met was two hundred years old. He was very, very angry and very, very horrible.

I began to understand that the Luggnaggians don't like the Immortals. They don't want to live for ever. Perhaps that's why the Luggnaggians are so happy.

***

After three months at the royal palace, I decided to leave. It was time to go back to England and my family. The king was sorry. 'Stay here,' he said. 'You can work for my government.'

'I'm sorry,' I answered, 'I must go home. I must see my family again.'

The king was very kind. He gave me some gold and a beautiful red diamond*.

In early May, I left Luggnagg. I arrived in Japan two weeks later. In Japan, I began to look for a ship to take me to Europe. It was very difficult to find a ship. After a few weeks, I found a Dutch ship. I spoke to the captain.

'Where are you from?' he asked.

'Holland,' I answered. The Dutch and the English weren't good friends at this time. It was better to be Dutch. Luckily, I knew the Dutch language very well.

jealous wanting what other people have
miserable very sad
spot
diamond

Captain Theodorus Vangrult was happy to take me. He needed a ship's doctor. I invented* some stories about my family in Guelderland. No-one knew I was English.

***

In June, we finally left Japan. The journey was long, but there were no adventures. We stopped at the Cape of Good Hope. This time, we only stayed for two days, because the weather was good. We got fresh water and sailed away immediately. On 6th April 1710, we arrived at Amsterdam. I immediately found another boat from Amsterdam to England. Four days later, I was home.

My wife was very happy to see me. She was very well and so were my children.

***

I stayed at home in England for five very happy months. Then, I started to think about travelling again. I spoke to some friends.

'Didn't you sail on the *Adventure*, a few years ago?' one of them said.

'Yes, why?'

'Well, they need a new captain. Why don't you speak to the owner*?'

I travelled to Portsmouth to meet the owner of the *Adventure*. After many years as a ship's doctor, I understood navigation very well. It was time for me to become the captain of a ship. The owner was happy, he remembered me from before.

'The job is yours!' he said.

I was very pleased. Now I needed a ship's doctor. I found a young man: he was very good at his job. Then, I said goodbye to my wife and children. We left Portsmouth on 7th September 1710. Our destination? The South Seas, again.

---

invent (here) say something that isn't true

owner if something is yours, you are the owner of it

Reading Comprehension

1 **Are the sentences true (T) or false (F)?**

		T	F
1	Lagado is bigger than London.	☐	☐
2	Lord Munodi likes the professors in the academy very much.	☐	☐
3	The dean is happy to show Gulliver the academy.	☐	☐
4	The professors have a lot of money for their studies.	☐	☐
5	One professor takes sunlight out of carrots.	☐	☐
6	There are some very clever people at the school of languages.	☐	☐
7	Gulliver decides to go back to Europe.	☐	☐
8	Gulliver meets some philosophers from the past.	☐	☐
9	Gulliver likes the Immortals.	☐	☐
10	French sailors take Gulliver back to Europe.	☐	☐

Speaking - Pair Work

2030 Agenda

Goal 4: *Provide Quality Education*

2 A **Discuss the following questions with a partner.**

1 How old are children when they start school in your country?

2 What time do lessons start and finish?

3 How old must you be if you want to leave school?

4 Do children have to pay to go to school in your country or is it free?

2 B **Search on the Internet for the following information.**

1 What does SDG stand for?

2 How many countries are working towards these goals?

3 How many goals are there?

4 Goal number 4 is to 'Ensure inclusive and quality education for all and promote lifelong learning.' Why do you think this is important?

Writing and Speaking ◆ 21st Century Skills

3 A Gulliver met Hannibal, Julius Caesar and Aristotle. Which three famous people from the past would you like to meet? Make notes in the box.

I would like to meet:
(1) .... , because ....
(2) .... , because ....
(3) .... , because ....

3 B Talk in pairs. Compare your answers.

Pre-Reading Activity • Chapter Six

Speaking

4 A Here are some events from Chapter Five. Why do they happen? Choose A or B and discuss your answers in pairs.

1 Gulliver makes his final journey to another country. Will he visit
☐ **A** an imaginary country?
☐ **B** a real country?

2 Gulliver meets two groups in the next country. Will he meet
☐ **A** men who are kings over horses?
☐ **B** horses who are kings over men?

3 Gulliver enjoys his life in the new country. Is it
☐ **A** because it's a peaceful country?
☐ **B** because the country is often at war?

4 Gulliver goes back to England. Is he
☐ **A** happy to go back?
☐ **B** sad to go back?

4 B Read Chapter Six and check your answers.

In the Land
of the Houyhnhmns

Pirates attack me. I meet some Yahoos.
I live with the Houyhnhmns. I return to England.

▶ 9 My journey to the South Seas as captain wasn't very good. Some of my men died on the way to the West Indies. I stopped at Barbados and the Leeward Islands. We needed some more men. I made a bad choice: some of the new men were pirates. There were fifty men on my ship. The pirates talked to my men. 'We can take the ship and kill the captain,' they said.

'We can make a lot of money for ourselves,' my men thought.

'I don't want to kill the captain,' one man said. 'He's not a bad man. But I agree, let's take the ship.'

One morning, twenty of the men came into my room with guns. Now, I wasn't the captain, I was a prisoner* on my ship. They gave me food and drink, but I had to stay in my room. I stayed in my room for weeks and weeks. The pirates took the ship past Madagascar.

***

One day, the pirates put me into a boat. They took me to the shore and left me. Where was I? I had no idea. I sat on the beach. I had some money and some gold in my pockets, but no food or water. I tried to think. 'I must find some people,' I decided.

prisoner someone who isn't free

I got up and walked away from the shore. After a while, I saw a line of trees. Through the trees, I could see some animals. They were very ugly indeed. They were very hairy and some of them had long beards. They could walk on two legs, but they were like monkeys. Some had yellow hair, others had red hair and others had black hair. They were *almost* human, but I didn't like them at all. I hated them as soon as I saw them. I didn't know why.

Then, the animals saw me. One of them came up to me. I was scared, so I took out my sword. The animal shouted and about forty others ran to help him. They threw things at me. Suddenly, the animals all ran away. I turned round to see why. There was a grey horse walking into the field. The animals were afraid of the horse. The horse was a little surprised when he saw me. He looked at me and walked around me. We looked at each other for a while. I put my hand on his neck. The horse didn't like this: he pushed my hand away with his leg. He made a strange noise and a brown horse appeared. The two horses both made noises.

'They're speaking to each other!' I thought.

The two horses looked at me again. They looked at my coat and hat. In their language, they said a word – *Yahoo*. They repeated this word three or four times. I was a little scared, but communication is important.

'Yahoo!' I said back to the horses.

They were surprised.

'Houyhnhmn,' said the brown horse.

'Houyhnhmn!' I repeated.

The horses talked together for a while. Then the brown horse left. The grey horse pointed at the road with his hoof*.

hoof the foot of a horse

'He wants me to go with him,' I thought.

I walked onto the road and the horse followed me.

We walked for about three miles. Then we arrived at a big building.

'Good,' I thought, 'I'll meet the horse's owner.'

I was wrong. Inside, there were other horses, one was very young and one was its mother. 'Yahoo,' said the mother, when she saw me. I was confused*.

The grey horse understood. He took me outside. There, in a field, was an animal. He pointed at the animal with his hoof and said, 'Yahoo!'

The Yahoo was just like the animals on the road.

'This horse thinks I'm a Yahoo!' I thought. 'I'm quite similar* to one, except* *they* are very dirty. *They* have no clothes. *They* are very hairy. I have nice clothes and I am clean, but I look a little like a Yahoo. I have feet like a Yahoo, except I'm wearing shoes.'

The grey horse looked at me and looked at the Yahoo. He seemed pleased and said something to another horse. That horse brought me some food. It was disgusting*. I couldn't eat it, so the horse threw it to the Yahoo. The Yahoo ate it greedily*.

The horses were kind. They wanted to give me food, so they brought me some of their food. It was too dry. Luckily, they brought some milk and I was happy.

That night, I slept well. I didn't sleep in the field with the Yahoos and I didn't sleep in the building with the horses. I slept between the two.

***

The grey horse was my owner. He wanted to teach me his language. He wanted to understand more about me. Every day, the grey horse and

The Yahoos are like humans and through them Swift shows that he doesn't agree with the Enlightment culture of 18th century England that had a positive opinion of humans and what they could do.

confused you feel confused when you don't understand something
similar almost the same
except but, only
disgusting not good
greedily quickly, wanting more to eat

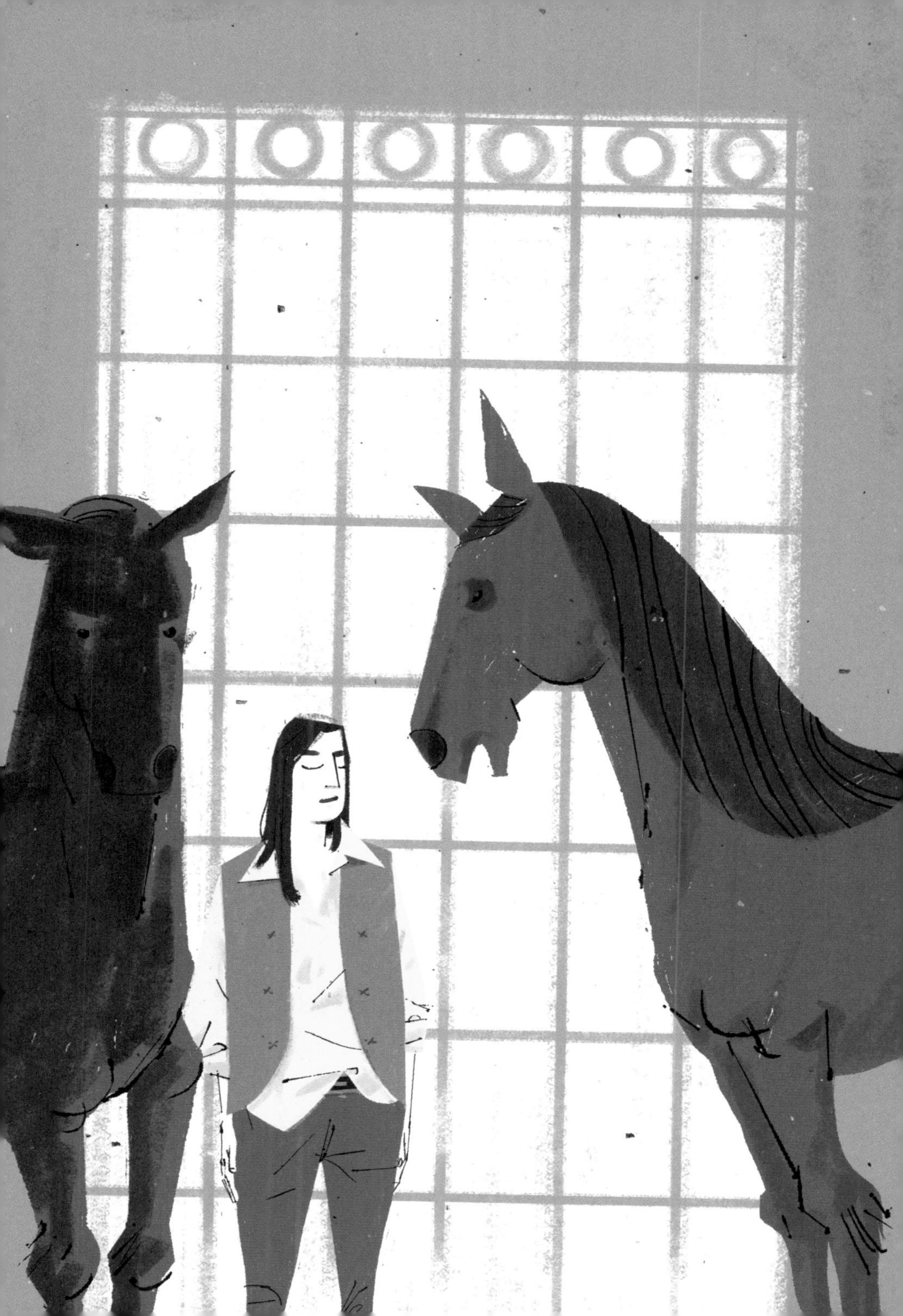

a little brown horse gave me lessons. I wrote words down to help me remember them. The horses didn't understand. They had no books and they couldn't write. After about ten weeks, they were surprised, but I could understand their language. The word 'Houyhnhmn', in their language, means 'horse' and it also means 'perfect'.

One day, my owner asked me some questions. 'Where do you come from?' he asked.

'Another country, across the sea.'

'No, you're wrong,' said the horse. 'There are no countries across the sea.'

He asked more questions. 'Do you have Yahoos in your country?'

'Yes,' I answered, 'they're the rulers* of our country. They're called *people*. They're different from your Yahoos because they're clean, they wear clothes and they can write.'

'Hmm. And do you have Houyhnhmns in your country?'

'Yes. They're called *horses*. They work in the fields. People look after them. Sometimes people sit on their backs.'

The grey horse was angry.

'It's different here,' I said. 'Here the Yahoos work in the fields. There, horses work in the fields.'

***

I talked to the grey horse every day. He began to understand about my country. But he didn't understand the concept* of war. 'Why do you have wars?' he asked.

'For a lot of different reasons*,' I answered.

'How do you fight? Yahoos aren't strong.'

'We have guns and swords.'

'This is terrible,' he said. 'Europeans are more vicious* than Yahoos.'

ruler a leader or a king
concept idea

reason why you do something
vicious very bad and dangerous

The horse was also sad when I told him about our strict laws, because they don't need laws in the land of the Houyhnhmns. He didn't like our money system – there are no rich people and no poor people there. He was shocked when I talked to him about the diseases* we have in Europe.

***

I learned a lot about Houyhnhmn culture. I was happy and healthy* living there. They're very peaceful. Houyhnhmns like to be friendly and kind. They have no negative words in their language (except for Yahoo). Education is very important to them. They teach their children to be clean and to work hard. Physical activity is very important to them. They must be strong and fast. Young Houyhnhmns run up and down hills. Every three months, there's a competition* of running and jumping.

Houyhnhmns don't write, but they like poetry. They know a little about astronomy. They're never ill. For small accidents*, they have very good natural medicines.

The government of their country is very important. Every four years there's a Great Council*. The senior Houyhnhmns all go to the Council. It lasts for six days. There, they make important decisions about food, Yahoos and family.

***

I stayed in the land of the Houyhnhmns for a long time. One year, there was a Great Council. My owner was the Member of the Council for our area. He told me all about it when he came back. 'We had one important debate* about the Yahoos. Some Houyhnhmns want to kill the Yahoos.'

disease something that makes you ill
healthy not ill, very well
competition when you do something with other people to see who comes first

accident when you hurt yourself
Council a political meeting
debate when people talk about their different ideas of something

'Why?' I asked. 'Houyhnhmns are peaceful. You don't kill animals.'

'No, but they're noisy, dirty and dangerous. You're different from all the other Yahoos. You're intelligent. You've your own language and you also speak ours. You're clean.'

'Thank you,' I said.

The grey horse didn't tell me everything about the Council. Later I understood more.

***

I was happy. I loved my life with the Houyhnhmns. I began to walk a little like them. I spoke only their language. I had a small house. I made a bed, table and chairs for myself. I made clothes for myself. My food was very simple and very good. I made bread and I found honey* in the forest. I had no problems. Here, there were no criminals*, no politicians*, no stupid people, except Yahoos. Sometimes I went to dinner with the Houyhnhmns. We talked about love, nature, traditions* and poetry. Sometimes I thought about England, my family and the people I knew in Europe. 'Yahoos,' I thought. 'They're all Yahoos.'

***

One morning, the grey horse came to see me. He was sad. 'You must leave us,' he said. 'You must return to your country and leave the land of the Houyhnhmns.'

'No!' I cried, 'I am so happy here!'

'You must go. I didn't tell you everything about the Great Council. Members of the Council are very angry, because you live with me. You live like a Houyhnhmn. You don't live with the Yahoos. They're afraid of you.'

'Where can I go?' I said, sadly.

honey bees make honey
criminal bad people: the police stop criminals
politician a person who's part of the government

traditions things that a group of people do or believe in

'You can't swim back to your own country. Can you build a boat?'

'Yes,' I answered, 'I can build a boat. But I need time.'

'I understand. I'll tell the Members of the Council that you need two months.'

He was sorry. I was *more* than sorry.

I made a boat from a tree. The little brown horse helped me. We made a sail*. We made paddles*. We prepared food and water for my journey. Finally, the day arrived. I had to leave the Houyhnhmns and my wonderful life. The family all came to the shore to say goodbye. Many other Houyhnhmns also came.

'Goodbye,' I said in tears*. 'Thank you. I'll never forget you.'

I kissed the grey horse's hoof.

'Goodbye,' said the grey horse.

'Take care, good Yahoo!' said the little brown horse.

I pushed my boat into the water and left the land of the Houyhnhmns.

***

My desperate* journey started early in the morning. The horses stayed on the shore. Sometimes I heard the little brown horse, 'Take care, good Yahoo!'

Finally, I couldn't see them anymore.

I wanted to find a small, deserted* island. I was in the South Seas, there were many islands there. I didn't want to return to England. I stopped at one island, but the people fired arrows at me. One day, I saw a ship. I was afraid because I didn't want to meet any Europeans. I sailed to a small island. I put the boat behind a rock and waited. I was unlucky. The ship sent a small boat to the island to get water.

sail a thing you use to move a boat in the wind

paddle a piece of wood for moving a boat

in tears crying

desperate very sad

deserted with no people

They found me and my boat. The sailors were from Portugal. They saw I was European and they asked me lots of questions. 'Where are you from?'

'England. I'm a *Yahoo* from England.'

They didn't understand the word Yahoo. 'Why are you here?' they said.

I told them my story. The sailors were very kind. 'Come back to the ship,' they said. 'Our captain will take you to Europe.'

'No! No!' I cried.

'He's mad, poor man,' said one of the sailors.

They took me to the ship.

***

The captain of the ship was Pedro de Mendez. He was a very gentle* man. He listened to my story. I was afraid of the sailors – they were dirty Yahoos. He was quite clean. The journey to Lisbon was very comfortable. Pedro de Mendez was very patient with me. He helped me a lot. He took me to meet his wife and children in Lisbon, but he repeated one thing, 'You must go back to England. You must go back to your wife and family.'

In December 1715, I finally arrived back in England. My wife and family were very happy to see me after so many years. At first, it was very difficult for me. 'They're Yahoos,' I thought. 'Dirty, horrible Yahoos.'

***

Today, my relationship with my wife and children is much better, but I still have problems with some Yahoos here. I bought two horses as soon as I got back. I speak to them for about four hours every day. They understand me quite well. They live in a nice building near mine. They're clean and beautiful. They're kind to me and friendly to each other. I love Houyhnhmns.

gentle kind and calm

Reading Comprehension

1 **Choose the best answer A, B or C.**

1 What do the pirates do?
- ☐ **A** They try to kill Gulliver.
- ☐ **B** They leave Gulliver in a canoe.
- ☐ **C** They leave Gulliver on an island.

2 What do the animals look like?
- ☐ **A** They're ugly and hairy.
- ☐ **B** They're ugly and grey.
- ☐ **C** They're hairy and fast.

3 Why do the animals run away?
- ☐ **A** Because they're afraid of Gulliver.
- ☐ **B** Because their leader calls them.
- ☐ **C** Because they're afraid of the grey horse.

4 What's a Yahoo?
- ☐ **A** An animal with a long tail.
- ☐ **B** An animal which catches fish.
- ☐ **C** An animal which is similar to a human.

5 Houyhnhmn means horse. It also means
- ☐ **A** beautiful.
- ☐ **B** hard-working.
- ☐ **C** perfect.

6 Why does Gulliver have to leave the Land of the Houyhnhmns?
- ☐ **A** The other Houyhnhmns are afraid of him.
- ☐ **B** He attacks a Houyhnhmn.
- ☐ **C** The Yahoos don't like him.

7 How does Gulliver feel in London?
- ☐ **A** He's happy to be home.
- ☐ **B** He prefers the company of horses.
- ☐ **C** He wants to travel again.

Writing

2 **Complete this travel guide using words from the box. Use the illustrations in the book to help you remember.**

> unusual - kind - happy - small (x2) - distracted - peaceful - poor - famous

Lilliput is an island in the South Seas. The people are **(1)** ....
Brobdingnag is an island near Lilliput. There's a channel between the
two islands. The people on Brobdingnag are also very **(2)** ....
Another interesting place to visit is Laputa. This is a very **(3)** ....
island of Balnibarbi. The people on Laputa are very **(4)** .... and
the people on Balnibarbi are very **(5)** .... It's a good idea to visit
the academy on Balnibarbi, but take some money because the professors
don't have any. They need it for their studies.
If you're travelling from Luggnagg to Japan, it's a good idea to visit the small
Magical Island. If the king likes you, he'll call ghosts of
(6) .... people from the past. A very interesting experience.
You could also meet Immortals in Luggnagg itself, but they aren't very
(7) .... people.
Finally, all travellers to the South Seas must visit the Land of the
Houyhnhmns. The Houyhnhmns are very **(8)** .... ,
(9) .... people. If you visit them, you won't want to leave.

Speaking   21st Century Skills

3 **Work in pairs. Discuss the questions.**

- Did you enjoy Gulliver's Travels?
  Why/Why not?

- Which characters from the book
  did you like? Why?

- Which characters from the book
  didn't you like? Why?

Jonathan Swift

Born in Dublin in 1667, he's one of Ireland's most important writers.

1667

Family and Education

His father died before he was born so he grew up with his mother and sister. His uncle, Godwin Swift, helped the family and paid for Jonathan's education. After getting his degree at Trinity College in Dublin, he moved to England.

1694

Early career

He worked as a secretary to diplomat, Sir William Temple, where he met famous people including the king. He also met a girl called Esther Johnson who he called 'Stella' and helped her with her education. In 1694, Swift became a priest and went back to Ireland.

Writing

Swift returned to England and helped Sir William Temple to write his autobiography. Then he returned to Ireland and became Dean of St. Patrick's Cathedral. Stella moved to Ireland to be near him and Swift started to write and publish political satire. In 1704, he published *The Battle of the Books* and then *Gulliver's Travels* in 1726. In 1728, he wrote a satirical novel called *A Modest Proposal* about the poor people in Ireland. He became a hero in Ireland for this book.

1716

Friends

Swift was friends with other famous writers of that time like Alexander Pope and they had a club for writers called the *Scriblerus*. Some say that Swift married Stella in 1716. Nobody is sure but she was very important to him and he published *Journal to Stella*, a collection of his letters to her about politics. In 1727, when Stella was very ill, he visited her often but he was too sad to go to her funeral when she died in 1728.

1745

Final years

Swift continued to write political satire, letters and poetry. In the last three years of his life, he became very ill. He died in 1745 in Dublin and is buried next to Stella in St. Patrick's Cathedral. He left all his money to start a psychiatric hospital in Dublin that still exists today.

CLIL History:
Exploring Australasia

Europeans travelled all over the world during the Age of European Exploration. They made very good maps of many other continents. One of the last areas they explored was Australasia. The main explorers in these areas came from Holland, France, Spain, Portugal and England.

WILLIAM DAMPIER REACHES AUSTRALIA.

Terra Australis Nondum Cognita

At Swift's time, Europeans knew about most of the world's continents. One area they didn't really know about was Australasia. Explorers knew about the Philippines and Indonesia. Sailors also knew there was a big country in the South Pacific. On old maps, there's a place called *Terra Australis Nondum Cognita* (unknown land of the south). It was quite easy for people to believe that there was a new continent to explore.

Abel Tasman

Dutch travellers and explorers were probably the first Europeans to arrive in Australia. They wanted to find the new continent. They travelled a lot. They bought things from people on other islands in the South Seas.
These people bought things from them, too. Abel Tasman was the most famous Dutch explorer of the area. He discovered a small island very near to another big country. He called the island Van Diemen's Land. Today, this island is called Tasmania. Then Tasman sailed around the larger country. He called it New Holland (modern day Australia). Many other Dutch explorers visited New Holland and Van Diemen's Land. They still believed that there was a bigger continent in the south.

William Dampier

New Voyage Round the World was the most popular book of 1697. Jonathan Swift read it and talked about it in *Gulliver's Travels*. The author was William Dampier, an English pirate, explorer and naturalist. The book was about his journeys, including his time in the South Seas. He especially wrote about New Guinea and New Holland. He wrote notes about the plants and animals of New Holland. He also wrote about the indigenous people he met there. When he returned to England, people were very interested.

He became captain of a ship called the *Roebuck*. He had one mission; to travel back to New Holland and explore it. The king paid for the ship. When he arrived in New Holland, Dampier wrote more notes about plants and animals. His secretary drew pictures. They also made maps of the areas they visited. Dampier wrote another book in 1703, *A Voyage to New Holland*.

Captain Cook

In 1768, Captain James Cook began to travel to the area. People still thought that there was an unexplored continent in the area around New Holland. He travelled a lot around New Holland and made very detailed maps. He gave names to many places, including Botany Bay (he had a botanist on his ship). He also made very good maps of New Zealand. Many people think he discovered Australia – they're wrong!

Antarctica, Terra Australis?

People gradually stopped thinking about a big unexplored continent south of Australia. They didn't start thinking about it again until 1820. In this year, a Russian, an American and a Briton all saw a land further south. Everyone disagrees about who was the first to see it. That land is now known as Antarctica.

Task - Internet research

Do some more research about one of the explorers on this page. Complete the form.

My explorer is ....
He was born in ....
He was born on ....
His first journey started in ....
His ship was called ....
He visited .... and ....
He's famous for ....
He died in ....

Problems at Sea

Was it difficult to travel round the world in the eighteenth century? Yes, there were a lot of problems: we meet some of them in *Gulliver's Travels*.

Pirates

The period from 1650-1730 is called the 'Golden Age' of piracy. Most pirates worked in the seas around the Caribbean. Spanish ships sailed from Central and South America back to Spain via this area. The Spanish ships were usually full of coffee, silver and other valuable things, so pirates were very interested in them. Most of the pirates were Dutch, English or French. Another area full of pirates was the area around Madagascar. Here the pirates wanted spices – also very valuable. Of course, pirates were dangerous, they stole anything they wanted including food and drink. Sometimes they killed the sailors, sometimes they didn't.

Longitude

Sailing at the time of Gulliver's Travels was very difficult. Today things are simple with global positioning satellites. On ships then, it was difficult to find places. Sailors needed to know latitude, altitude and longitude to find their location. Altitude wasn't a problem and they knew latitude from the position of the sun. To find longitude, sailors needed to know the right time. Ships at the time used watches, clocks and hourglasses (see the picture). There were many competitions to design the best way of calculating longitude. One eighteenth century invention, called a practical marine chronometer, was very important. This invention made it possible to tell the time correctly on ships. Sailors could then find longitude.

Weather

There were no engines on the ship, so the wind was very important to sailors. It could also be a problem. Ships at the time could only really sail with the wind behind them. It was usually difficult to sail into the South Pacific from Cape Horn, because winds came from the east. Ships had to sail along the coast to an area where winds came from the west. Captains often thought it was better to travel round the Cape of Good Hope into the South Pacific. The problem was the weather there: the old name for the Cape of Good Hope was the Cape of Storms. Of course, a ship couldn't move if there was no wind at all. In the eighteenth century, things began to change. There were new designs for ships and sails. It became possible to sail into an easterly wind. It also became possible to sail in bad weather. But there was still no solution for a day with no wind.

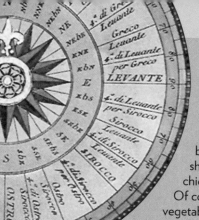

Conditions on Ships

Journeys were very long. As you can see from Gulliver's Travels, sailors were at sea for months. Conditions on ships were often terrible. Ships carried a lot of food – and a lot of mice. Perhaps that's why it was lucky to have a cat (especially a black cat) on ships. In fact, there were often animals on ships: chickens, sheep and even cows.

Of course, food was terrible. There were no fresh vegetables and no fruit on the ship. Sailors also worked very hard to sail the boat and to keep it as clean as possible. The pay for sailors was terrible. Many of them didn't want to be sailors, but had no other work. It's also important to remember that some ships were unsafe. Many broke up in storms.

Disease

A ship's doctor like Gulliver was a very important person, because sailors were often ill. They often didn't get enough vitamin C, because they had no fresh fruit or vegetables for long periods of time. This causes 'scurvy' and many sailors died of scurvy. There were also problems because ships were dirty and had too many people and animals in a small area. Sailors spent more time cleaning than sailing, but it was common to have diseases like cholera or typhoid on ships. Sailors also got diseases like malaria or yellow fever, when they travelled in tropical areas. Of course, they also gave European diseases to the people of the places they visited. In some places, whole towns full of people became ill or died because of explorers and traders from other countries.

Task - Internet research
Find the answers to this quiz in the texts.

1 When was the Golden Age for pirates?

   ....

2 How did ships calculate longitude?

   ....

3 What was the old name for the Cape of Good Hope?

   ....

4 Name a common disease of sailors.

   ....

Test Yourself

1 **Answer the questions about *Gulliver's Travels*.**

1 What's the name of the first country Gulliver visits?

....

2 How do the little people stop Gulliver from attacking them?

....

3 How does Gulliver escape to Blefuscu?

....

4 What's different about the people on Brobdingnag?

....

5 How does Gulliver get up to Laputa?

....

6 What's the problem with the professors at the academy on Balnibarbi?

....

7 Name one person from history that Gulliver met on the Magical Island.

....

8 Why does Gulliver hate the Yahoos?

....

9 Is Gulliver happy or sad to leave the Land of the Houyhnhnms? Why?

....

2 **Match the words to their definitions.**

1 ☐ a field	**a**	A verb meaning to speak in a loud voice.
2 ☐ the coast	**b**	A place where farmers grow things.
3 ☐ shout	**c**	A person who fights for a country.
4 ☐ owner	**d**	The part of a country near the sea.
5 ☐ healthy	**e**	If something is yours, you're its ....
6 ☐ a soldier	**f**	If you aren't ill, you're well or you're ....

Syllabus

Level A1

Articles

a, an, the

Nouns

countable and uncountable, plural, possessive

Pronouns

subject and object, indefinite

Quantifiers:

some/any, more

Adjectives

possessive, opinion

Prepositions

place, time, movement, phrases, *like*

Verbs tense, aspect and form

Present Simple, Present Continuous, Past Simple - regular and common irregulars, Future with *will*, *-ing* forms after verbs and prepositions, *can, must* for obligation, *need* for necessity, imperatives, *have got, would like*, common phrasal verbs, *there is/there are, know, think, hope etc + that clause, like/don't like + ing*

Adverbs

frequency, manner

Conjunctions

so, before, after, when

Young Adult **ELI** Readers